Decision-making and problem solving

Alex   Plascencia

Decision-making and problem solving

DEDICATION

This book is dedicated to all those people who for some reason stopped believing in themselves and did not find how to solve any problem that ocurr them, here you will find a logical point of view, created from a personal point of view, which you can take to your professional part as parents, legal guardians, director or owner of a company, manager, executive, salespeople, no matter your profession, even if you are a student can give you a better way to see things.

This course was created it at the end of 2013-2014 for a group of executives who were in charge of me in a financial, in which I held the position of zone manager, that I gave to the task of involving them, I knew that they would not, if it were a course, for reasons of ego, lack of knowledge of the subject and something that you will always find on a daily basis , they will always judge you without really knowing and less with foundations, eye this is repeated anywhere in Mexico, believe that for more than a year working in the field, they will always believe that they know everything, they will find a certain "Victor" who believes more than any individual, or a certain "Oscar" who has the potential but does not like to leave his comfort zone, , their character was part of their problem, intelligent, their security based on the ego, it was the only rescue of the group, the others followed their life according to their scope, some changed over time, it was an achievement to introduce this subject in a practical way and I am proud since they never realized for their egos.

Decision-making and problem solving

CONTENT

THANKS

To you, my beautiful redhead who supported me in difficult times, deciding that this course **was** necessary for your campus, was the first time that the staff in charge of it could be given training.

INTRODUCTION

This work aims to be a support for you Dear Reader, this in order to improve the quality of decision-making. It is well known that daily we make decisions... The question here would be how accurate and assertive am I in decision-making?

That is why doubts arise, a little uncertainty and sometimes we become somewhat hesitant, this because we want our decisions to be the right, correct and timely. It seems simple, but it really is not, because with each decision-making it is adequate or inadequate it will always generate a positive or negative consequence directly proportional and in order to the decision that was made.

Without further time and waiting will be of great use for your day to day in your personal and work life, in this way I start the first exercise as a start of the theme in vogue.

RETROSPECTIVE EXERCISE

Before starting with the theoretical part I consider is important and at the same time relevant to start with an exercise, which although, will put us thinking, reflecting and generating a little introspection, since it aims to see pre-test and post-test results commonly applied in specialized careers in research area. This is how we expect to finish effectively and efficiently this work that we can use as a tool of our daily life.

Next: Fill out this exercise before continuing with the topics, at the end of this book, you'll do the exercise again and compare it, you'll find differences and improvements.

RETROSPECTIVE EXERCISE

1.- What do we mean by making decisions at the personal - business - work level?

2.- What is your decision-making process?

3.- Under what criteria do you land your daily decision-making in the workplace and personally?

4.- Do you know the impact that a good and bad decision has in the workplace or personal?

Examples

5.- What is the appropriate decision-making process relevant, timely and effective?

6.- What is your process in handling a difficult situation and how do you solve it?

7.- What has been your biggest challenge throughout your work and personal life?

8.- What is the purpose of which you will mark yourself after reading this book?

Introspection moment ...

- When you make a bad decision, you are able to acknowledge your mistake.

How many times do you recognize?

How many times do you repair the damage?

How many times are you actively looking for other solutions?

Each person is different, each person has a different profession and varied criteria for his decision-making process and the impact of the solution to the problems we face day by day from the personal and family side to the positions we hold, with multiple responsibilities and obligations...

CHAPTER 1
PROLOGUE

First of all, let me tell you that I am not telling you how to make decisions, it is clear that you have a life making decisions, in this book you will find the right methodology and process using the right scientific method to this process, many people can make decisions logically, that does not mean that it is the right one or that has the best result, we face every day numerous decisions and large or small problems that we have TO solve.

This is where you have the ability to take on any personal or work responsibility when taking any position rasp held to re rout to solve problems and make decisions, two of the most difficult areas of professional work.

Solutions are often sought by reaction rather than prevention of problems; this creates more problems or constant problems because someone is not responsible during their job management or personally refuses that responsibility.

It is very important to take into account the teamwork for decision-making when you are alone, maybe you have a partner, in the work part you have a team with which you have the concept and the vision of several people to reach the best decision; to form teams you have to take into account the skills, commitment and responsibility of each of the members, in order to become a real team.

"Like it or not, the very essence of taking responsibility is in making decisions."

All the decisions you have to make are *decisions* with some degree of uncertainty, this creates emotional doubt, out of control and this generates terrible decisions, that's why it's important to focus and start from scratch, the problem is already there, so take your time to start analyzing, remember that you may have a solution and you don't know, when you have experience of the item in question, your own experience I could guide you, if you need more we will have to investigate and start untangling those ideas that generate indecision by the haste of the situation, that's where your experience and knowledge is worth, just give time to think.

Looking for information and working completely on the search by analyzing the alternatives and their possible results, we will not know the consequence of our decisions until we make them.

"When a decision is made it on the basis it is unlikely that we will fail."

If you do not think properly of the situation of the problem, nothing that guarantees that the conditions under which the decision was made remain the same, since we are in a constantly changing environment; although those taken without prior analysis, at random, are more exposed to failure than those who follow the proper process as I mentioned earlier.

Every moment of your life and situation in it is taking a risk; you have to identify the risks that each activity entails and take the necessary measures to minimize any problems.

(Decision-making and problem solving)

YES   NO

Taking risks is positive to learn from the successes and failures you will face, this will give you the common sense and experience needed to solve any problem.

Good decision-making allows you to live better, this is because you have more control over your life.

As parents, legal guardians, director or owner of a company, manager, executive, salespeople, etc. You have to make many decisions every day, some of them are routine or inconsequential decisions while others have a very strong impact.

Why some of these decisions might involve the gain or loss of goals you've set yours

CHAPTER 2
EVERY DECISION COUNTS

Every decision we make can be right or wrong, so we have to learn from our mistakes, decisions are like a double-edged blade, because both generate an apprenticeship.

The ability to make decisions always leads to risks, being creative and looking for alternatives to problems or challenges that are not yet existing.

"The accumulation of experience is long and sometimes very expensive."

The more you learn it is by the mistakes themselves, achieving a high level of experience requires time and knowledge with foundations and foundations for both your daily life and the world of work.

In decision-making we have to take into account:

- Future effects: In the short or medium term, decisions must be made on qualitative and quantitative basis, the one that a decision must be made in the short term cannot be underestimated and therefore less attention, this could lead to long-term problems due to a bad decision not adequately intended just by making a decision if to value things.

- Reversibility: This is when a decision can be reversed and the difficulty generated by lack of fundamentals is immediate, so you always have to make decisions with bases and foundations.

- Impact: This is when you need to think well, very well because it can last little or years because it doesn't give it the required importance.

- Quality: As long as the quality of work exists, ethical values, being within the foundation of law and legality.

- Periodicity: Decision making becomes frequent or continuously, as fires are extinguished every day.

- A frequent decision does not limit its value as opposed to a continuous one that is generated by bad decisions from different areas, which is that decisions must be made by assessing them according to a high or low level, that will depend on the situation.

- In summary:

High-level decision-making: It will require a process of analysis, search for alternatives, planning, execution and evaluation.	Low-level decision-making: They require little effort and little time.
Decisions affecting the future	Decisions that don't affect the future
Hard-to-reversible decisions	Reversible decisions
Broad-impact decisions	Decisions with little impact
Decisions affecting relevant quality factors	Decisions that affect few factors relevant quality.
Exceptional decisions	Decision that is made frequently.

CHAPTER 3
TYPES OF DECISION

Decisions can be Scheduled, Routine, or Inconsequendent:

Scheduled or routine.
Example: scheduled would be when you have the monthly expense and you have to pay the rent, services and pantry. On the work side, when the HR department has to schedule employee payments, rent payments, electricity, etc; A definitive methodology has been developed to be able to manage them, they have guides or sequential steps to solve a problem.

Unscheduled Decision: "These are those that require immediate attention because of your risk," you have to assess your low-risk or high-risk immediacy.

They are given little time for forgetting aspects such as the planning and the proper process mentioned above, having all responsibility for the decision, this means *ability* to *respond* at the time of a decision with foundations which are overlooked, generating proactivity, deciding to act at the moment, generating more problems and losses.

Many times you will encounter people who just observe and expect things to happen, without deciding, is acting irresponsibly, looking for a responsible one.

A reactive and proactive person acts on the basis of what happens to him, they foresee absolutely nothing, every decision is forced at the moment and they always present a single alternative.

When you are proactive, you have multiple alternatives to decide as long as you base with bases, otherwise it would be a complete mistake.

CHAPTER 4
ELIMINATE YOUR COMFORT ZONE

Anything that is outside our comfort zone, is difficult to see and even harder to try to get out of our comfort zone, this change can be difficult, with many doubts, painful or just frightens us.

Here comes a big forward question:

How do I know something new is better if I don't know it? the answer is: you won't know if you don't try. So go for it!

We all crave something better and we want it without looking, the opportunity we can have, maybe it is knocking on the door, but you do not know how or why, you just want to get it, that is where you are afraid to leave your comfort zone.

When you leave your comfort zone, you enter uncomfortable terrain, uncomfortable at first, but when you see that things weren't as you saw it, and that you now feel looser being out of your comfort zone, you discover the possibility of reinventing yourself and growing in unexpected ways.

The insecurity or anxiety that was generated while you were in your comfort zone, caused uncertainty, that's what often limits decision-making.

Managers with bad practices always find little time to solve difficult situations (problems), looking for who solves the problem or seeing who will be the culprit in addition to looking for saving formulas, ensuring wakeers, if this worked in the past, it was only because it generated more problems and solving the problem by blaming someone, solving a problem with a d'ddning decision, possibly sacrificing a good element rather than being responsible for their lack of direction and decision-making.

CHAPTER 5
HIGH-LEVEL DECISION-MAKING PROCESSES AND STAGES.

The process should follow the following methodology:

As an individual or on the job side you must have a basis of personal values in addition to academics according to the level of decision-making.

You always have to have Information: have all the data of the problem invogue, taking into account the objectives to be developed to define research with qualitative and quantitative elements.

Analytical capacity: Generate a qualitative and quantitative process to find solutions without neglecting intuition.

 Experience: In this case every person through work and personal experience is gaining knowledge, this can guide you to solve the problem.

Having the information, generate an analysis, based on your experience using you:

Academic or Research Knowledge: It is important to have foundations on the subject, being empirical can generate or aggravate a problem by ignoring the fundamentals, research on the subject

Once the previous 4 elements have been gathered you will be able to generate a:

Judgment: Use your judgment and common sense, using information, analysis with your experience, and knowledge to make the right decision.

CHAPTER 6
SNINGING A PROBLEM

Stages	Objectives	Skills needed
Identifying the Problem Explain the problem	Understanding the problem: What is it, why, when?,where?, understand the situation and context	Analysis Synthesis Global vision Critical Thinking
Devising the strategy How many Alternatives Deciding which strategy Designing the solution	Create a strategy A fundamentally supported solution that minimizes negative effects and ensures real achievements.	Creativity Negotiation Communication
Developing a way to solve Assess achievements	Achieve solution of the problem, also allowing the transfer and accumulation of the knowledge learned.	Leadership Empathy Teamwork

CHAPTER 7
IDENTIFYING SOLUTIONS

Detecting problems/opportunities can be very easy or very difficult, it will depend on your skills to anticipate a problem in time and be prepared to appear by mistake of third parties or ours.

Experience marks that problems can be instantaneous.

- ☐ The problem arises at the moment
- ☐ You have a preventive process and possible solutions.
- ☐ Generate opportunity at each solution of the problem.

Preventive process anticipates problems and leave it solved.

Corrective process is at that moment where you lose control of the situation which causes disorientation, this causes bad decisions generating a low performance that leads to stress and motivation.

In the day-to-day real life, problems arise at different times of the day "are around us", this is because someone is not making the right decision, everything is generated in chain and do not wait to be discovered.

In order to anticipate the problems, you must have a basic structure as we saw above and give them the value they deserve or take advantage of turning the problem in our favor by detecting areas of opportunity or simply generating an advantage of the problem itself.

For this it is necessary to develop a professional and individual attitude, and then work it as a team in an open way paying attention to everything around us, observe changes, stay alert, be a little reserved before making comments, structure your ideas, for many curiosity is a factor that I could generate problems, do not be so curious because you can make decisions without foundation (gossip) , stay tuned, be objective all the time.

The information of the topic in vogue is the foundation for making decisions, as long as you are better informed and truthful, decisions will be made with greater acuity and agility.

"The secret to making decisions is in truthful and timely information always well-founded"

You have to make decisions in a focused way, you can't be a judge and part you have to make the decision coldly with enough basis, follow the process mentioned above, you won't find the black thread of things, would be enough to improve the way in how to make decisions.

You should never be guided by unfounded or without sustainable basis or unsubstantiated words generated by personal egos of third parties. (Friends, Co-workers, family).

Generally bad decisions are generated by letting you be guided by third parties, far from helping you can make it worse, generating a very delicate situation, in which the only beneficiaries will be them.

That's why take your time follows the processes mentioned above, make them your own so put into practice, the most difficult decisions are usually simpler to solve, but they get complicated when you don't have the right information, these devising possible factors without first, looking for a foundation, basis, analysis, experience and judgment.

CHAPTER 8
PROCESS TO IDENTIFY PROBLEMS AND HOW TO SOLVE THEM.

1. What is the problem?

2. Context and real situation of the problem.

3. Analysis of the situation and the problem.

Fund the analysis, have all the information, investigate thoroughly on the subject, look for similar situations within your experience and how you solved it, investigate similar situations and how they were resolved.

You can assamble a file with all the information, this can be done personally or by working as a team; dividing the search for data, organizing everything is essential, this will determine your assertiveness in the resolution.

Once you have made the complete file on the subject and why the problem occurred, you will be able to assess the intensity of the problem, whether it is low risk or high risk, having all this data it is very easy to make the right decision.

The way to establish the solution of the problem will be clear and well-informed, the problem will have several options in terms of solving it.

The cold and objective mind allows you to have a better mink of the moment and the problem, giving you enough time to create the "file" (like a well structured mind note) with everything related to the problem and be able to use it in future either as a solution or example in a training, this can be used to define strategies for a personal purpose or increase your goals in the work area.

CHAPTER 9
HOW TO KNOW IF YOU'RE PART OF THE PROBLEM AND HOW TO FIX IT.

Something that I rather like to do during the courses that I give to everyone, should do a SWOT (Strenght, Weakness, Opportunities, Threats) in a personal way and another in a way of work, I will tell you why. Because this it allows me to have a complete X-Ray of the participants (to know them better) and how they perform at work, much base their decisions as if it were a family issue and the other way around, that's when you may determine that they're part of the problem, by not making decisions based on the work side, they automatically continue the same process to their daily lives.

Then they wonder why everything happens to them? and the truth is because they do not put the type of decision and responsibility in a job dividing the personal part, in Mexico we used to follow the flow, a wrongful (unwarranted) decision-making at an operational level (People with basic and elementary studies.) to means commands (They are those who are those who are middle higher education) , and very rare that a senior manager (Managers, Directors, Owners of their own businesses, etc.) has this type of problem since it is more accustomed to decision-making, without involving the personal part.

In the latter section with the high commands, it is very rare or difficult that may it happens, although it actually happens and even more. So when government they put people in positions that do not have the training and academic development of the area, or they have a very advanced age to be able to make an effective decision because of their lack of updating their knowledge or experiences.

Managers who have no idea how to manage, manage and less lead a team, will always have organizational problems, such as anecdote; I have come across managers who are doctors and their only preparation is in medicine, completely failing the administrative part, having the following medical problems since Alzheimer's making decisions of which he does not remember the decisions corresponding to his position, thus forgetting important administrative data – doctors, which ultimately generates an impact in definitive, not positive to his performance , impacts on your work staff and thus patients or users of the facility of which (the doctor with Dx. Alzheimer's) * directs.

- *The previous paragraph is a mere example that actually happened in my professional experience with a partner who sadly was diagnosed with Alzheimer disease, his position in the company was blessed not because of his talent, because of his "important friends" from the gov.*

  He actually refused to gave up on his job even though he was aware of his mistakes, bad choices, terrible consequences of his (wrong) decisions, and he couldn't care less for the people who were paying the consequences of his errors, he pretended to be just fine even when he saw the result of his actions; part of this was mainly his ego, he didn't let it go, so he was kind of irresponsible, was so proud that he did not care about the others and the impact of his decisions and actions. On the other hand, this example is just pretended to be illustratative also to invite you to be responsible in your decision process and let go the ego and be less proud, those things may let your mind quite cloudly that you won't be able to see the things how it should be, neither clearly. So be wise in your choices and try not to affect badly the others...

This X-Ray of the participants and in this case you, you will have to make one to see your strengths and weaknesses within the workplace and as a person, will give you the tools to grow.

As you will notice this tool is very, very useful to get to know you better and know your weaknesses at work and not be part of the problem, doing this the answers to the problems will become more and more successful.

Weaknesses	Threats
Strengths	Opportunities

*Dx.- Abbreviation referencing diagnostics.

In a notebook sheet or for printing, you will divide the sheet into four, remember that it will be 2 exercises one will be to know the professional part and the other will be the personal part, in the end you will have two sheets divided into four as shown in the diagram.

You have to be very objective to get to know yourself:

WEAKNESSES: What are your weaknesses in your work/staff, you are the only one who knows them, you were honest with yourself.

THREATS: This is where you'll sweat because you have to recognize what your threats are at work as a staff.

STRENGTHS: Put all your strengths, you know them backwards and right.

OPPORTUNITIES: Here you will have to put what your options would be for both work and personal improvement.

There are more techniques to detect problems, I will tell you which ones I have used the most:

Making a box to know and delimit the problem consists of the following:

Nature of the problem (Where it exists) and (Where it does not exist).
Locate the problem (Where, zone or geographic extent, place).
Magnitude of the problem
Type of affectation It's low or high priority
Options *a-b-c-d-e-f* to fix the problem with basics.

CHAPTER 10
ANALYZING THE PROBLEM

Importance of the problem by making a pretrial on the significance of the issue in vogue/opportunity to achieve after solving the problem

Limits of the problem, this is because we already know its immediate consequences giving rise to the limit of the problem, giving the opportunity to manage it properly.

Always keep in mind the consequences and causes limiting the problem once we know clearly with the consequence of the problem, when analyzing the causes of it we will set a general picture.

Using the URIM technique delimiting the problems between urgent and important, subclassifying within them the problem, resulting in resolution and classification types.

Urim		Urgent	
		-	+
Important	+		
	-		

At this point it is very important to define decisions based on limiting the actions to be taken, for example:

In a company that sells prefabricated furniture you have to decide to start the project and have everything ready to execute it, the cycle begins with an executive who sells the project, estimates are given to the customer in real time, when it will be the delivery of the furniture that requested, implying all that this entails (contract of purchase sale, advance or total payment of the furniture.) Etc.

It follows the process of assembly in production area where the executive must deliver a copy of the contract, to begin the production process, *in this inter many* things go wrong by different factors, communication, monitoring and proper solution by both parties, the client only expects his furniture on the agreed date, there is so much bureaucracy within the company that cancer is generated from every company, I call it *"mailitis"*, that this, they all want to *solve it with pure mail*, looking for those who have the best foundation or excuse to withdraw from their true functions, begins the hunt of the one who is wrong, by egos all fall into bad practices before the owner finds out why the client already asks for his financial return , and this generates more expenses, incredibly believe that it is solved with extra gifts, because you have a very high margin and do not see what is important, at the end of the day someone is to blame and fired or just give up so much "screwed up". (this is my very own point of view) *.

From a secretary looking to grow up within the company that generates questionable subjects, to zone managers who want to treat everyone like well-behaved children but I'll play that in another book.

Mailitis (Neologism own): like an illness; unnecessary bureaucracy to respond within a company, all areas use this inefficient method, misuse mail, using it as a distraction of functions and problem solving. (Poor performance and safe losses with this process).

They don't see the losses for two things: one for the very high profit margin and the 2nd. by the uns suitable staff for each area, common situation in family businesses where the doorman ends up being the plant manager after 10 years.

As you can see there is already a very big problem within the company and with the customer.

I leave you a possible solution table:

I recommend doing the exercise based on your experience and knowledge, you will see that there is more than one solution for everything.

Urim		Urgent	
		-	+
Important	+	Unnecessary mails, wasted time	Delivery of the furniture on an agreed date
	Solving internal problems	Give away items for bad work, part of the profit given by company errors.	Control of any area to be able to have immediate access for out-of-time production.
	Delimit subjects to put work order for your assembly process.	Work based on egos.	Eliminate egos at work, have the right staff and not promote staff who don't have the profile, no longer you've been in the company, that will never create efficiency, just problems. One thing is trust and another is his true vocation.

CHAPTER 11
ALTERNATIVES ANALYZED FOR
DECISION-MAKING.

One decision is to choose, from a series of possibilities, the best of them generating a solution to the problem, every day you will meet people who do not think first before deciding or worse, act without first thinking the result of their actions.

That is why before taking action you have to gather all the information and ideas generated, start working on them until you find the right ones.

What do we do with all that collection of ideas that have appeared in a creative session?

Which one of them do we choose?

What will be the most effective problem-solving strategy?

It is important to note that over time you can have a strategy to be able to solve any problem, everyone who created it according to their way of being or the way they work.

You always have to make an assessment of alternatives and decision making according to the following criteria which you can enrich with your common sense and experience.

- Looking for our benefits through estimated goals, what do we gain?

- Creating an analysis and chances of success what is the probability of achieving it?

- What is it up to us to get it up and running or not depends on some internal or external factor in the company?

- What means could we need? (people, materials, etc.)

- Estimated time.

- What does it mean, besides what risks are we going to take?

If we finish the evaluation of alternatives, without finding one that is really satisfactory, something you are not doing well or you are part of the problem, seek support, we cannot abandon the problem simply because you are part of it, there will be other people who can help you.

As important as the problems are, however difficult, give yourself time to find suitable, viable and effective solution.

CHAPTER 12

TECHNIQUES FOR VALUING AND MAKING DECISIONS

If you read the book you will know that they are qualitative and quantitative and all you have to do is a spreadsheet with the above to generate your own way of solving the problems that are there, waiting to be solved with real knowledge and foundation, from your personal and work foda, you *know that "foot limping" and* you know which areas you should work for your personal growth, the factors mentioned above, structure them according to your experience, way of being, but what will never change will be :

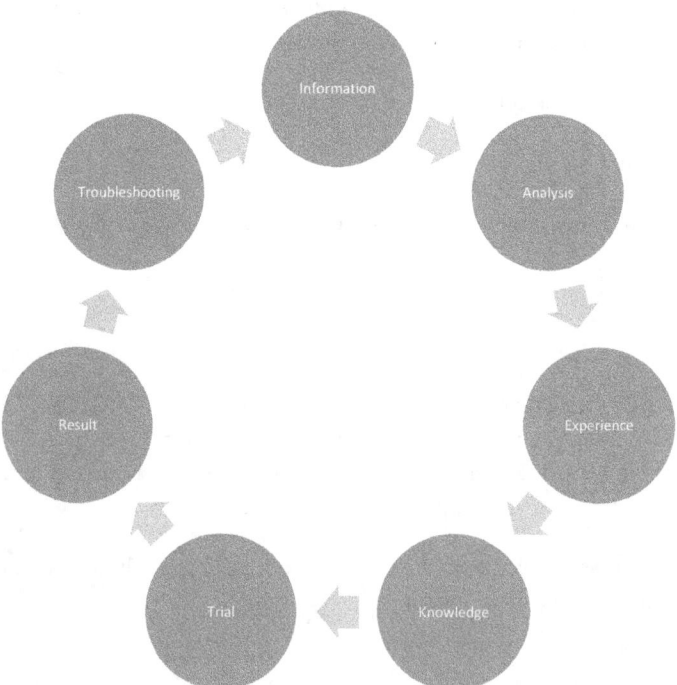

Remember to have different options, make the next panel to solve the problem with different options.

CHAPTER 13

HOW TO GENRE ALTERNATIVES?

This table is simpler than it looks, mentally you can do it in times of prompt action, example.

In daily life is occupied every day, check out this example:

When we go through the pantry, mentally we know where to buy things, we don't always buy everything in the same place, this is because we seek to save on buying pantry in the super market when we actually know where to buy certain things in different places looking for savings, there are supermarket chains that allow you to buy products by volume, allowing you to increase the savings in the pantry of certain items that can last more than a month , as it is to buy liquid soap for clothes, when purchased in volume, it automatically becomes savings because it is a bimonthly purchase.

The example that is on the next page is very simple, it is something that we do every day, the difference is that it is organized, increasing the efficiency in saving the pantry, every day we try to make the best decision, where to buy cheaper, where to search for quality and price, at all times we make decisions, the difference is in seeing this , organize the decision-making process, how many times you have not heard to say, I am late, I could not, I do not know how to do it, when we really have the answers for our own questions, the most common question is Why me?, it always happens to me, this is because we do not see that we are part of the problem by not organizing our way of making decisions.

Exercise table: In this table it can be informative, in turn that this can be used as a basis for everything from the handling and emptying of qualitative or quantitative information data, this will depend on the use, that is how this resource can be used in a personal and / or work way.

Alternatives Strategies	A Criteria	B Efficiency	C Profitability $	D Required technology and legal sustainment	Total
A					
B					
C					
D					
Total					

STRATEGIES AND ALTERNATIVES

Alternatives Strategies To compare	To Criteria	B Efficiency	C Profitability $	D Required technology and legal sustenment	Total
To Shopping Center 1 call yourself Wolmort	Buying some items, exclusive sale	10min purchase time	Just buy the necessary items, store with high costs	Online orders just to pick up	10% of the purchase super.
B Shopping Center 2 call yourself Cotcenter	Purchase of products in volume and quantity.	Purchase time from 10 min to 1 hour	Purchase of non-perishable and perishable food all of excellent quality x excellent cost savings per volume.	Online orders 10 min, store tour 1 hr	80% of super purchase
C Gas stores, all of them	Buying commodities	Purchase time from 5 min to 15 min	Basic purchase soda	No online orders	5% purchase of the super for being occasional or daily
D Traditional shop	Buying commodities	5 min to 15 min to buy	Basic purchases or for the only place where they sell the product.	No online orders	5% of the super comparison for being sporadic or daily purchase.
Total	4 different places to achieve the full purchase of the store / market	Between 5 min of purchase to 2 hr during the purchase process,	Significant savings when buying the pantry.	Save time when buying online and just pick up the order.	100% of the purchase process, deciding where to make the purchase improvements

As you can see, it's something we do on a daily basis, we just don't go through a proper process, we do it mentally in a disorganized way.

CHAPTER 14

HOW DO I CARRY OUT THE PLAN AND GET IT UP AND RUNNING?

Here is the most important moment, launch and execute action plans in the face of the problems that we live daily such as the previous exercise in which we saw personally the diagram, in the work we will find that, there is not always the approval of the immediate boss for reasons of company policy or by pure arrogance and ego of this individual. It's okay to see that you are part of the solution will take you into account and most likely with the other bosses say that he was the one who put the idea and you developed it, as is the case, which is something that will benefit the company.

This is where you already have the basics to approach your immediate boss and give him an essential point of view that he doesn't see for people who just act like they work and don't perform as they should be; is so it turns out to be a good time to grow up and give an irrefutable point of view for the way you did things, well done and with foundations.

Try to sell your proposal to solve what generated the problem, after fixing it is easier, since you will have all the support to not happen again, to make decisions in a company, it is because the charge requires it, if you are from another area sees with feet of lead, there are many "scavenrgers will feel attracted to steal your ideas".

In personal life, in everyday life we will see things more clearly and above all we will be more informed than others, who only like to say things without thinking, just to have the last word, even if you do not believe it in some medical cases with studies, usually come to confuse basic and elementary concepts such as: melancholy , a healthy and passing sadness with the diagnostic concept of depression (mood disorder see DSM-V) is where you will realize how good a doctor he is, curious, isn't it?

Since just mentioning this has called into question his ability as a doctor, in addition to his knowledge, I tell you why, the only ones who can determine a depressive state are psychologists, clinical psychologists or psychiatrists through a variety of psychological and neurological evaluations in a specific way, a general doctor without the aforementioned specialties could not diagnose anyone with depression , without having the basics that the area of psychiatry must do, personally only makes them look bad, it seems more like a gossip and generates problems or collateral situations not favorable to those who receive a verdict as such, because when it presents a lack of foundations it cannot be called diagnosis.

"Now you'll have the tools to disarm any absurd and non sense answers."

CHAPTER 15

DEVELOPING THE INTERVENTION PROCESS TO SOLVE A PROBLEM

As we saw in the previous topics we have a process to be able to make more effective decisions let us call it the first phase where we understand and understand the problem in all its complexity; we can distinguish between symptoms, signs, causes, in addition to knowing what the next causes and remote causes would be, as well as possible alternative results, with different decisions that encompass the solution of the problem.

During the analysis and synthesis, not only an explanation but a model was developed to guide the intervention, through the aforementioned processes.

You have to search for information, organize it, analyze it and then synthesize it to know how it influences the problem and discards low-impact solutions.

Second phase emphasized the creation of different alternatives as we saw in the example tables above, so that we could rely on strengths (FODA), minimizing obstacles, creating fundamentals to solve the problem.

You will have new professional skills that will help you solve any problem, from low impact to high impact, because at this time of the process you will have increased your creativity, innovation, imagination, reaching the metacognitive process, linked to the examination of the processes of reasoning and expression themselves, commonly called common sense.

Third phase solving the problem by applying the complete methodology of this book.

On the work side you have to develop an action plan and those who will intervene in it, for a company it is important to work as a team to solve the problem.

The following questions can help us begin the process:

- What are the five most important measures that need to be taken to implement the troubleshooting programme?

- Who should be, in an essential way during the decision-making process, providing their knowledge and experience in addition to being committed to the implementation: managers, supervisors, all those who involve the problem?

- How should these measures be communicated to solve a problem?

- Control of unforeseen events that could occur during the troubleshooting process.

- Present short- and medium-term solutions in addition to the problems generated by the problem and what is the estimated loss.

Every company or decision maker must create and organize their own team to find the best decisions. To be a leader during this process you must have the foundations and knowledge, a lot confuse leadership by intervening without knowledge, believe that encouraging are leaders, that does not work, on the contrary, it is very likely that there are many problems within the company, being this leader part of the problem by not being propositivo with foundations and knowledge.

FINAL CHAPTER

EVALUATION OF THE ACHIEVEMENTS GENERATED BY YOUR PROMPT ACTION TO SOLVE THE PROBLEM.

This is the last stage of the problem solving process is marked by having all the information, analyzing it, this will lead you to be able to decide better, at any time in your life or at work, because it is important this sequence, well having all the information is not organized are individual elements that form the information as such, which begins to have organization in the analysis , giving different solutions with different margins from profit to times, giving rise to different ways of seeing the problem with different variables to solve the problem, organizing the entire result of the information and analysis you can make the best decision in the appropriate area, solved the problem from different angles.

To evaluate the decision-making process is closely linked to improving every moment and with the learning left by the troubleshooting process, which I was able to help in the immediate future because it is cyclical, there will always be a problem to be solved.

Don't become "fire extinguishers", making decisions that only save the moment, you have to eliminate the bad processes and organize everything from scratch.

"It's up to you to improve the way you can solve any problem in your life, just organize your thinking, structure the steps to follow, have the basics, research, get all the necessary information, analyze and act."

ABOUT THE AUTHOR

It is a pleasure to be able to introduce myself to you Dear Reader, my name is Alex Plascencia, with the career in Business Administration, this course (handbook) was created to generate, increase and improve results in a team work group, in my 20 years of experiences in Administrative and Management areas allowed me to see the opportunity to improve the field of work and teamwork, which allowed me to continue studying the area of Human Resources Management , which significantly marked an improvement by allowing me to create courses to train my staff, which many have succeeded and others continue to ramble in monotony and not because the course or book does not work, they simply did not make the decision to use what they apparently learned, as they continue to "always" make informed decisions, having to resolve the consequences of their bad decisions when they were able to make a proper and informed decision in their time , because they are considered "badass /know – it-all" (but not) when they have neither the foundation, basis, experiences and knowledge, so they are damned to continue deciding by hunches.

Thank you for reading this brief, but concise book, I hope that from now on your decisions will be thought out and organized.

www.ingramcontent.com/pod-product-compliance
Lightning Source LLC
Chambersburg PA
CBHW070519220526
45467CB00002B/755